D0743117

Farmyard Friends
COWS

Maddie Gibbs

New York

Dedication: *For my father, because cows do wander*

Published in 2015 by The Rosen Publishing Group, Inc.
29 East 21st Street, New York, NY 10010

First Edition

Editor: Caitie McAneney
Book Design: Katelyn Heinle

Photo Credits: Cover, p. 1 smereka/Shutterstock.com; p. 5 steverts/Thinkstock.com; p. 6 Matthew Jacques/Shutterstock.com; pp. 9, 24 (calves) Fuse/Thinkstock.com; p. 10 David Maska/Shutterstock.com; pp. 13, 24 (horns) Leena Robinson/Shutterstock.com; p. 14 Robert Crow/Shutterstock.com; p. 17 Peter Bay/Shutterstock.com; p. 18 Dr Ajay Kumar Singh/Shutterstock.com; p. 21 Blend Images/Shutterstock.com; p. 22 Symbiot/Shutterstock.com; p. 24 (cheese) Sea Wave/Shutterstock.com; p. 24 (yogurt) tacar/Shutterstock.com.

Library of Congress Cataloging-in-Publication Data

Gibbs, Maddie, author.
 Cows / Maddie Gibbs.
    pages cm. — (Farmyard friends)
 Includes index.
 ISBN 978-1-4994-0083-0 (pbk.)
 ISBN 978-1-4994-0086-1 (6 pack)
 ISBN 978-1-4994-0082-3 (library binding)
 1. Cows—Juvenile literature. I. Title.
 SF239.5.G55 2015
 636.2—dc23
                              2014025283

Manufactured in the United States of America

CPSIA Compliance Information: Batch #CW15PK: For Further Information contact Rosen Publishing, New York, New York at 1-800-237-9932

CONTENTS

Cows 4

Kinds of Cows 12

Useful Animals 23

Words to Know 24

Index 24

Websites 24

Cows live on farms. People raise them for meat and milk.

Cows on a farm are often called cattle.

Male cows are called bulls.
Baby cows are called **calves**.

A cow's stomach has four parts. It breaks down the food a cow eats.

Texas is famous for its longhorn cattle. They have long **horns**.

Angus cattle are polled.
This means they have no horns.

Highland cattle are furry.
They are from Scotland.

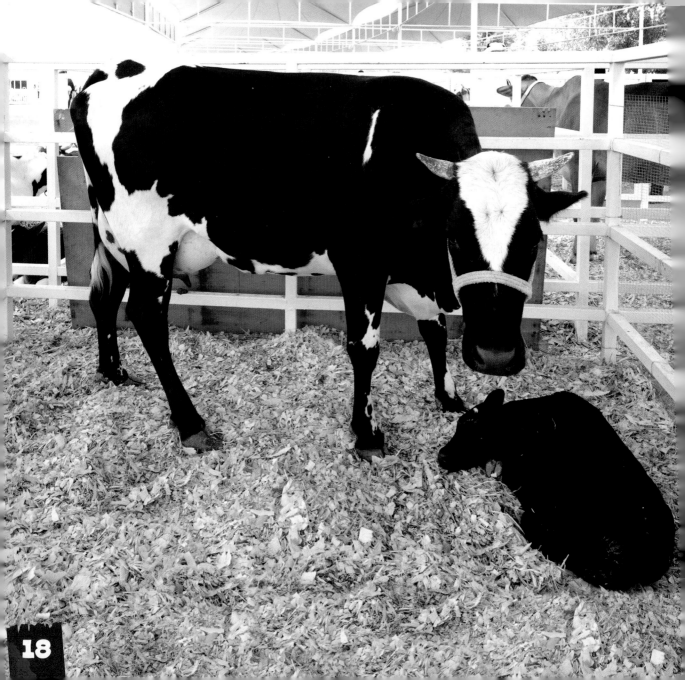

Holsteins are dairy cattle.
They are raised for their milk.

People drink cow milk. We also make **cheese**, **yogurt**, and ice cream from it.

Cows are useful animals.
Have you ever seen one?

WORDS TO KNOW

calves

cheese

horns

yogurt

INDEX

B
bulls, 8

C
calves, 8

H
horns, 12, 15

S
stomach, 11

WEBSITES

Due to the changing nature of Internet links, PowerKids Press has developed an online list of websites related to the subject of this book. This site is updated regularly. Please use this link to access the list: www.powerkidslinks.com/fmyd/cow